The Secret Psychology of S

By

Joseph A. Caulfield

Revised &

Edited Version

ISBN-13:

978-0615585017 (Joseph A. Caulfield)

ISBN-10:

0615585019

Chapter One

Knowing That You Don't Know

What's stopping you from closing sales you should be closing?

You may have felt this question gnawing at you for some time, and now you're beginning to earnestly investigate. It is why you're reading this. You may have figured out that there's a lot more to the game of selling than meets the eye.

You've been missing data, and you know it.

Knowing that you don't know is extremely valuable. It is the launching pad for any new abilities and a personal evolution of thought.

I believe that it's not you, and "No," it's *probably* not your product.

What is it then that may be stopping you?

It is:

Not understanding the mental constructs of a prospect in a sales situation, coupled with the lack of a great sales process to facilitate decision-making.

The BIG questions for you are·

- DO you want to get a grasp of newly recognized automatic "mental reflexes" that stop improvement of closing ratios?

- IS it useful to understand the mental constructs occurring behind the scenes?

- IS your understanding that a necessary component of sales is continuing education?

If you can answer "yes" to any one of these then... Let's get started.

This book is short, but every word, every phrase will be important to the whole of this work. Pay attention, and look for ways to connect the dots as you read, both in sales and with your real life. Any data is only as good as it works, and any data studied needs *you* to make it successful. Many others have made this data work in two different sales teams, so you are not a pioneer, but you are an early-adopter.

Simply said, there are psychological issues that need to be addressed before many prospects are even able to purchase. If not answer the prospect slips into procrastination and hesitation on consummating a deal.

Other questions answered here are:

- What prospects really buy?

- How informational sales presentations prevent you from helping prospects in the most effective way, and stop many sales.

- Why you are not achieving trusted advisor status?

- Why these new skills, will help you facilitate the prospects' ability to make a buying decision NOW.

Chapter Two

Sleight of Thought Trick

One sleight of thought trick is to act in a manner different from what the prospect's expecting. Prospects have come to expect certain behaviors from sales people. As an example, enthusiastic presentations are one of those behaviors, along with justifications, and defenses of product or service. It can be very irritating, if you're the prospect..

Think about it for a moment. If you're feeling down yourself, and someone comes up to you in wild enthusiasm, what's your reaction? Not good I'm betting. Let's say you just found out you lost an account you thought was in the bag, and someone sweeps into your office full of cheerfulness – how do you feel? How do you feel toward them, at that moment?

In the sales process itself prospects generally swing between two major mood levels. Sometimes they're very positive – ready and eager to listen, and sometimes very negative – *they don't see a need for you or your service.*

It's considered normal to try and move the prospect in the direction you want them to go. This, however, is exactly the behavior the prospect's expecting, and they're mentally prepared for it. Mentally prepared to block you. This, unfortunately, creates a competitive environment between you and your prospect.

Let the wars begin. It becomes a psychological tug-of-war.

Besides, can you recall what happens when any sales consultant tries to move a prospect in one direction, or the other - anyway? Nothing happens, generally speaking. The prospect either doesn't move at all, or goes below the mood level where they started. That's not good.

Here's the good news. We can use this tendency of a prospect's resistance to our advantage. Try this, it's like mental Judo – rather than directing the prospect in the direction you want them to go, push them in unexpected directions. Get moving in bold new patterns to avoid the prospect's conditioned response, which is often called social machinery.

Warning! This process will require you to withhold your own excitement and enthusiasm, and to stop talking about your product and solutions the first chance you get.

It demands that you not offer quick solutions for what you think is your prospect's need. This can be difficult to master; after all, you know you have THE answer. I don't want you to have 'THE' answer. I want you to have THE sale.

Chapter Three

The First Basic Major Mental Reflex®

The *"Earlier Similar Response Reflex"* is a Basic Major Issue you must understand to begin to grasp the automatic mental constructs of the buyer's mind, and Mental Reflexes® in general. This is huge. Let me explain.

When getting a physical, doctors always get out that little hammer and bop you just below your knee to check for good or bad "reflexes." Even if you consciously try to stop your leg from reacting, you can't. It is a reflex.

What has been discovered is that the mind has automatic reflexes too, and those reflexes effect sales. When the mind gets bopped, it's called triggering. This mental bop reanimates any similar history people may have in relation to what's happening in present time - automatically.

The mind automatically and *unconsciously* goes to any earlier similar history on what triggered it – if it wants to or not. As stated, chances are good to excellent that a lot of the content from earlier incidences is not even consciously available.

The mind remembers stuff from the past in its' quest for survival. It is like we've taken mental notes on everything that has happened in life and put them on a huge electronic post-it board, called the sub-conscious. So, if and when this subject matter, or something similar comes up again, we are prepared with awesome solutions.

Unfortunately, the answers from the electronic post-it board are not always right, as they are very often clouded by pain, stress, blame or regret within the past incidents themselves.

The next chapter exemplifies how this works.

Chapter Four

A "Walking Dead" Plot

If you sell workers' compensation insurance
and you're talking to a prospect about it, every
earlier time the prospect had any history about
workers' compensation, or the audits, fines and
claims connected to it are awakened back to
life – and the memories, including the emotions
from back then, become active on a less than
fully conscious basis. It's like a new kind of
movie – with a "walking dead" kind of plot.

Like it or not, the mind uncontrollably goes to
anything it has in its' electronic post-it data
bank that has to do with the subject matter
being discussed. It captures all past decisions,
and all the emotions connected to it, plus any
auxiliary items.

It **IS** how the mind works. The good news is
that we are all the same; we have discovered
it, and how to use this to our advantage.

The Secret Psychology... process applies
conscious critical-thinking skills to these not
fully conscious earlier similar instances. As we
shine a spotlight on them your entire sales
world changes for the better – and so does the
prospects.

_The Secret Psychology... process allows
prospects to make present time decisions_

without looking through the prism of past stressful events.

Selling methods (eventually) evolve based on findings in psychology and/or neuroscience. Modern medical scanning techniques now show us in living color and real time, information we've never known before on how we think – how we make decisions.

Chapter Five

Social Machinery

Understanding social machinery (conditioned response) is central to consulting. Social machinery is something we build internally to handle the everyday stuff – the mundane. All of us do it.

Surely, you have wondered when you see an associate who is having a serious bout with allergies respond with "Good" or "Like a million" to your question of "How's it going?" It's almost laughable.

It is the pervasiveness of conditioned response/mental reflexes that help create a less than finely tuned decision-making ability. That costs us sales, but only because we have not learned how to handle it – until now.

This short book and process will help your prospect dismantle some of that automatic conditioned response as it relates to their goals, purposes, and objectives.

Sales, marketing, and advertising people are always looking for ways to bypass social machinery, and get to the actual person, to get an emotional response. This is why you see ad copy that makes ridiculous statements.

It is all an attempt to shock or entertain potential buyers into present time. It's an effort to get by social machinery to tell about something new, so that you do not immediately reject it.

Mentally, social machinery/conditioned response is the gatekeeper to the inner self, emotions, and evolution.

Just to complicate matters, your prospects know that sales and marketing within their own company are responsible for their revenue. No company survives if it doesn't generate sales.

So, they read the same books you do and even attend sales seminars. They know the sales game, which is to say – *they have your playbook*. They're ready for you when you walk through the door.

Chapter Six
<u>Upgrade In Software</u>

Any great selling process must be easily learned, quick and interactive. It must also be personal, on a business level, and it's always informal.

Prospect participation is invited and demanded. After all, psychologically at least, you will be making an upgrade available for the prospect's thought software.

We need the prospects' involvement – their permission. So, if they refuse to participate, we thank them and walk away, thus ending the cycle on being unpaid consultants. We chalk this experience up as being with someone who did not match our ideal client profile. They've self- deselected.

The Secret Psychology of Selling, and the book *Rapid Sales Success* transforms sales into true consultancy.

Selling is defined as, "the activity of persuading someone to buy something," and that the word consultant is defined as, "An expert who gives advice?"

Business owner prospects are the same as the rest of us. They have some issues. Those issues delay their growth and stop them from achieving better outcomes, without them ever knowing it.

What we have are tools that encourage the use of their critical-thinking skills on any areas of upset.

The prospect determines where the upset is. It's not a consultant telling them what, or how to think. It's them taking a fresh look, by shining a flashlight on some issues they have just indicated that they would like to talk about.

Chapter Seven

The Mental Prison

When done correctly, the issues are desensitized, and we get the prospect into a very special place called now. In present time, unencumbered, a logical and sane decision can be made about purchasing. They are once again able to take independent action—independent from the mental prison of past pains. If the prospect buys your product or not you will have helped them tremendously.

We have been trained into believing that if you understand a prospect's problem, and provide a killer solution, the prospect will purchase. This is mostly false, as it is only true in about four percent of the prospects you call on. That is miserable percentage-wise, and keeps you working way to hard.

In the remaining 96% there are behind-the-scenes issues, which if not handled, become a tug-of-war between the consultant and the prospect. This is true even if the solution you offer is the best solution – the prospect is still saying "No," as they are blocked by past issues in the form of a bad gut feeling, or sink into an apathy engendered by their earlier similar anxieties.

Chapter Eight

Kicking and Screaming

Kicking and screaming (one of my favorite activities) over doing something entirely different will not improve closing ratios, and we all know by now that to continue doing what we're doing will just keep giving us the results we've become accustomed to.

The only way to shift the results to an uptrend is to do something radically different, something that bypasses your own social machinery, and then the social machinery or conditioned responses of prospects. People aren't lazy and no-account, they just have social machinery that says everything is okay, or worthless or pointless anyway, and the residual prism of past failure encourages people to just not try. The score? Prism = 1, Prospect = 0, Consultant = 0.

The *internal* decision-making issues that the prospect is confronted with must be addressed. Your future sales depend on you actually helping prospects navigate through this process. The good news is 35% + closing ratios. I have had people achieve over 50%.

This also could mean you do not need more appointments, more face-to-face calls, if you are closing more of who you are already seeing.

Chapter Nine

You Take the Blue Pill

Remember The Movie *Matrix*?

Keanu Reeves plays Neo and finds out that all of humanity is actually living in a computer-generated simulation called the Matrix... Like living in a dream.

"Reality" in the Matrix is what the program says it is, not what it really is.

At a critical part in the movie, Neo's mentor offers Neo two pills and says, "You take the blue pill: the story ends, you wake up in your bed and believe whatever you want to believe. You take the red pill: you stay in Wonderland, and I show you how deep the rabbit hole goes."

Guess which pill Neo takes? (I mean it wouldn't be much of a movie if he took the blue pill, right?)

So I ask you, would you take the red pill or the blue pill?

I'll tell you this; the reality you've been living in has been created by you, but unconsciously. The same is true for everyone. When you learn how to create reality consciously, everything changes. And I do mean everything. You can invite others to change their conscious reality, as well through this process.

For example... If you could create more sales NOW, instead of dealing with the lousy economy, the media keeps talking about, would you?

Well, you can.

I'm saying you can change what other people see, hear or experience - right now. I am saying you can change how they experience their business life. Look, there are a lot of ways to describe it, but they all boil down to this:

People have the ability to create their own experience of life, if they can get out of their own way.

You can too.

The power to CAUSE change in yourself and others is so life-altering that I feel humbled to share it with you.

As sales consultants we are successful to the degree that we can positively influence mental functions, and facilitate changes in behaviors that lead toward betterment.

Chapter Ten

Analytic System Check

There is a psychological phenomenon that tells the mind to discard or modify whatever does not fit within the minds own current reality. This should be ranked as super important. So, when anybody sees or hears something they don't understand, they explain it to themselves in ways that make sense to them.

Do you see the significance of this reflex?

I call this an *Analytic Substitute* – meaning the mind replaces something that is unknown with a mental image or concept that can be recognized – an analytic substitute.

We do this all the time, when we encounter things that we just don't get, we simply interpret it in ways that we do. Not understanding is uncomfortable, and our minds crave a comfort zone.

There's no conscious thought to Analytic Substitutes. It's automatic, and done in nanoseconds.

Question: If prospects process unknowns through this Analytic System Check, and come up with something that fits its' own current reality - but, which may not pertain to the actual reality of what is now being presented - would this affect your sales – Your closing ratios? The answer is YES!

Prospect's fill in what's unknown, with what fits...from their own personal "knowns" – their own reality.

For sales consultants this becomes a super-sized problem, as anything being explained that is outside of the prospect's experience keeps being modified to fit their current mental constructs.

The prospect assesses what they experience, but only within the terms of what it has already experienced – what it knows; it searches for a data of comparable magnitude. If there is none, it fills in the blanks. Can you say, "makes it up?"

It is easy to see how this becomes detrimental. While you're in presentation mode the prospect's mind is building its' own consensus reality, and then casts their consensus reality into cement – where it is concretized, *if it is correct or not.*

The sales processes of Rapid Sales Success Company, as represented in several different books defeats these reflexes, a.k.a social machinery and conditioned response.

In recent years, there have been companies trying to educate us on some of the known aspects of newly discovered mind-brain connections. When this subject is studied, however, you're left with the thought, *"What else don't I know?"* A list could be made that would be quite long.

Chapter Eleven

Frequency Following Response Reflex (FFR)

On that list would be "altering brainwaves technology." Spooky. The altering brainwave thing is interesting, because we (humans) discovered a *Frequency Following Response Reflex* that the mind and brain have that is nothing short of spectacular.

One of the incidences that led to discovery was the strobe light used in the old disco settings. They discovered that when someone who had epilepsy went to a disco they could easily have a seizure, all because of the strobe lights. This led to research that led to even greater discoveries and finally, the Frequency Following Response reflex. That has led us to many different modern products.

One small example: When you are feeling highly agitated your brainwaves go into a high beta frequency, or even a low to mid gamma brainwave frequency, depending on your degree of agitation. This is pretty uncomfortable. On an EEG, those waveforms would be very choppy, in contrast to smoother waveforms like alpha or theta.

When these 'choppy waveforms' of agitation are occurring, and you have a meeting in an hour where you should be calm, cool, and collected, you can now listen to a Centerpointe product and manipulate your own brainwaves. You are then good to go – calm and relaxed once again, in minutes.

The reason this technology works is because of the Frequency Following Response reflex the brain does, which simply means that when the brain is presented with a different, yet dominant waveform pattern from where it is currently at – it will match and follow it. It will synchronize. Now that is cool, and useful.

Once this was discovered that meant we could utilize it in many different ways for self-improvement products – like the company Centerpointe does.

I have not read anything that mentions sales, the immediate environment, plus brainwave technology. In practical terms, however, I have experienced a business owner respecting my request for a closed door and no interruptions, to include people or telephones. I want them in their comfort zone, with whatever their normal brainwaves are.

Chapter Twelve

A "Wants" Analysis

Keeping prospects focused on your product/service category called for the development of a tightly honed "wants" analysis that we call the Commonality of Issues Sheet (CIS) or Personal Inventory Assessment form. This easily constructed sheet keeps you and your prospect on track. It is a laser-guided solution for discovering decision-making anxieties that can interfere with your sale.

*Sell prospects what they 'want', but deliver what they 'want" and "need'. The reason is clear; people **always** buy what they want.*

A 'want' could be defined as a perceived 'need'. Your typical client may need what you sell, but your perfect client WANTS what you sell and buys it. This process helps the prospect see their own wants.

Chapter Thirteen

The Process

The Secret Psychology of Selling sales process advocated consists of ten steps. It was pulled from the books "Rapid Sales Success" and "Radical PEO Sales Success."

The steps used are listed here to give you an idea of placement:

1. Overview of the product or service
2. Commonality of Issues Sheet (CIS) – the "wants" analysis.
3. Recall System – shining the spotlight on pain w/critical-thinking skills
4. Gathering Data
5. Custom Presentation – built on the issues prospect has stated – only.
6. The Cost Box
7. Handling Objections
8. The Close
9. Client Calendar/Timeline
10. Referrals

I may have a few things, or none at all to say on each step. I am sure you have your own verbiage. I will comment only if I feel there are some 'secrets' you may want, or need to know.

Chapter Fourteen
Overview and Mind Maps

Step 1

In the Overview of your company/product, you can use a PowerPoint® presentation, or physically draw an umbrella on a blank sheet of paper and name the top of the umbrella "The name of your company." Below that write "Your company slogan."

The underside of the umbrella has labels placed on each side, separated by the umbrella handle. Those labels are the major points of sale for your product. What you are looking for is a graphic representation of what you offer, solution-wise, in a very simple picture format.

The choice of whether to use a laptop presentation versus a hand drawn picture would depend on the business setting. When presenting to a group, drawing may be difficult, but is always preferred because *it is not normally done, and so evades social machinery*. I have also found that drawing is a lot less intimidating. It has the added advantage of putting you next to your prospect. Most sales are a peer-to-peer sale.

The drawing itself is actually creating a **Mind Map**. A Mind Map is a diagram used to represent ideas linked to a central key word or idea. It is a tool that helps to create a conceptual understanding for your prospect.

Mind maps are used to generate, visualize, structure, and classify ideas, and as an aid in problem solving, and decision-making.

Mind Maps get the mental significance of your product out of the prospect's thought-software, and on the table for physical inspection and extrapolation (See Figure 1)

The Overview should accomplish two specific purposes:

1. To get the prospect in a buyer's frame of mind

2. As a Set Up for the Commonality of Issues Sheet

Step 2

The Commonality of Issues Sheet (CIS)

Here is what you say:

*"Let's take a closer look (Prospect Name), and quickly see if there's a potential fit with what I do. Over the years our industry has been in business, we've seen a Commonality of Issues that most business owners have regarding our product. Please take a moment and fill this out. **It has the added benefit of letting us both know if I can be of any help. If I can't be, I'll leave."***

Once you've done the Commonality of Issues Sheet, you'll have point specific issues that interest the prospect---their "hot buttons" i.e., their "pains." *Only discuss these issues* – they are the ones that are real to them. Do not discuss any other features or benefits.

I know, there are other bells and whistles that you offer, and the thought running through your mind is ---"Just wait until s/he sees____, (not on the list) s/he will really want our product."

This thought is your mind lying to you. You
are attempting to co-share your reality. Selling
is not about you it is about them.

While not appearing logical, *anything* you say
on any issue that is not checked as "Needs
Improvement" on the CIS (Commonality of
Issues Sheet) can open "Pandora's Box" and
will probably stop your sale. Your offering is
not rocket-science; let's not turn it into it. Stay
on the same reality page that your prospect
has already created. It is their "Top of Mind."

There are countless analysis sheets to
determine needs. My advice is to perfect and
simplify the CIS sheet continually, and save the
rest for later – much later. Most industries
have many different needs analysis sheets.
They range from a two-page document to a
six-page document. Why not use one of
those? They certainly are much more intricate.
The answer is that they would be a violation of
attempting to discuss what is NOT Top of Mind
with the prospect – not in their current field of
vision.

The Commonality of Issues Sheet (CIS) is
compiled from surveys done by telephone,
mail, or in person on your company's existing
clients, or on your existing clients. These are
clients that are currently utilizing your service
or product, and they're kind enough to share
their reasons for buying. Those reasons for
buying become your "Wants Analysis"(in
question form) that I call the CIS.

The Needs Analysis that is six-pages long is an
excellent tool for after the sale, but not in
making the sale. The lengthy Needs Analysis
would be a shotgun compared to the rifle shot

of the CIS. A needs analysis is attempting to uncover wants; we discovered your current clients have that information already.

The golden rule is: "Sell them what they want, deliver what they want and need."

Outlined below is a CIS (Commonality if Issues Sheet) that was done for a test industry. Once you've got the surveys done of your client base, it is easy to do for any industry.

COMMONALITY OF ISSUES SHEET (Example)

Most Business Owners-CEO'S Experience

In Control = IC

Needs Improvement = NI

	Please Check	IC	NI
Cost of Employees dollars lost from the bottom line?		___	___
Payroll. Job costing, timely, effective, accurate?		___	___
Are lawsuits/disputes frustrating and expensive?		___	___
Customer Retention...impact to your bottom line?		___	___
Audits: OSHA, DOL, Worker Comp		___	___
State Unemployment taxes in control?		___	___
401(k)?		___	___
Government Regulations:		___	___
HR is in full legal compliance?		___	___
Worker Compensation Modifier going up or down?		___	___
Terminations. Legal consequences?		___	___

Benefits too costly- time spent answering questions? __ __

Vision...does anyone share or participate in yours? __ __

HR Department...a profit center? __ __

Employee Retention. Working for your competitor? __ __

Chapter Sixteen
The Recall System

Step 3:

The Recall System is designed to get your prospect into unresolved issues that have affected cash flow, the company, and them personally. After doing the CIS, take each item listed by the prospect as, 'Need Improvement' and ask the following questions, in order.

This recall process presents the paradigm shift from sales to consultant, and will propel you to a trusted advisor.

Why do all of this? To invite the prospect to see things can go wrong, but then to show that we could have prevented or at least lessened the damage. This process nullifies social machinery, and encourages the prospect to apply their critical thinking skills to past anxieties that may be interfering with their current decision-making skills.

Purchasing anything is an emotional issue, so be empathetic, or you may lose the sale.

The Recall System:

"I see you checked_____as 'need improvement',

- "Tell me about that" (issue from the CIS they said, Needs Improvement)
- When was that?
- "What did that cost you?"
- "How did that affect your business?"
- "How did that affect you personally?"

- "What impact did it have?"
- "On a scale of 1 to 10 how committed are you to fixing that?"
- (If answer not "10") "What would make it a 10?"

If you do not get a "10" casually ask:

"Is there an earlier time this same sort of thing happened?" (A major question, when needed)

If there is an earlier time, go back to Step 1 and repeat the steps on the newly found item. If no, reinvestigate each pain given to assure that you have all of the answers. Be gentle and be conversational.

It is important to get all of the answers on each question. You may have to probe, while still being conversational. What you are looking for is the emotional response, and the commitment of a "10" to fixing it.

The idea here: After getting a "10", move to the next item checked off in the "Needs Improvement" area on the Commonality of Issues Sheet (CIS). Statistics tell us that if you get multiple different Issues, your closing percentages skyrocket.

Note: If you absolutely cannot get a ten do not belabor the point. Pretend you did and move on.

Do not present solutions at this stage.

Even though it's tempting. Often, it's the prospect doing the tempting. They want solutions. Have the courage and discipline to follow the process completely.

Know that people have a certain pride of ownership of their problems – prospects are no different. They have, after all, gotten used to these problems and they're familiar with them. If we jump all over their problems with an enthusiastically quick solution they will not take kindly to it. I know it makes no sense. Problems and eventual solutions must be coaxed from the prospect whenever possible - keeping them at cause, as opposed to effect.

Most business owners are skeptical of change anyway. Not just a little bit, but a lot. They've fought long and hard to be where they are, and they're extremely hesitant to change anything. And we all know that change is painful. Is solving a problem a change? Why yes, it is.

Current anxieties being experienced must overwhelm the dislike and discomfort of change for a prospect to act.

The Secret Psychology of Selling process emphasizes this and then allows them to safely act. The ability to change is a wonderful ability, but beware of its cousin "constant change". Change for change sake is an illness.

Our minds operate on a linear time track like an old videotape machine constantly moving forward. What was recently painful, quickly steps into the past, and then the distant past – and then, seemingly gone, Oh, it is still there, but you'd have to hit the rewind switch to find it – it slips into the electronic post-it board – unconsciousness until rewound or triggered. Our process is that rewind switch.

Step 4: Gathering Data

In many sales you must gather information to consummate a sale. It is valuable to collect all that is possible, prior to the closing. It is part of the assumptive close, and it gives you extra data to determine if you can sell this prospect. Collect this data quickly.

Step 5: Custom Presentations

After doing the overview of your industry, the Commonality of Issues Sheet, The Recall System, and gathering of data, you are now ready for a presentation that will have significant impact on your prospect. Now you can take what you know about the areas checked off as "Need Improvement" and be wonderfully creative.

This sales process is all about the prospect's issues, their business, and at their level of awareness. You have built a incredible custom made presentation, literally tailored for them.

Step 6: The Cost Box

Why do we fear pricing? Why is it that this one aspect is so overwhelming?

Because pricing is scary, and it's a bit overwhelming, but only if you have not done the Secret Psychology of Selling process.

You obviously have to know the numbers cold on anything presented. *Many times, part of that fear is simply you needing more comfort with your own numbers.*

Value-added selling is selling according to the prospects perceived needs (wants are perceived needs), as that IS what they value. It is discovering through The Secret Psychology of Selling process those things that the prospect perceives as real, and then coming up with solutions (value) to address those point specific concerns.

Your typical client NEEDS what you sell, but your Perfect Client WANTS what you sell.

Step 7: Handling Objections

If you've spent a few months selling your product or service, you have probably heard the bulk of objections already. We must become adept at handling these objections while appearing calm, cool and collected. We have to be actors.

You can also do a paradigm shift on the prospect, which is great fun. It is another 'secret.' When the prospect objects say, *"You know, I am not very good at handling objections – perhaps we can work through this phase together."* How is that for a paradigm shift?

Chapter Seventeen

Negative Reverse Objection Handling

Do this before you close, especially if prospects are not raising any objections. The unvoiced objection kills sales. You walk away, they think of an objection and stop the buying process.

Say this:

"(Business Owner), I have a few concerns that I would like to address." Then you unload, one at a time, every objection you can think of that they might have, and let them handle it. It is fun and effective-try it. It is another paradigm shift and totally evades all social machinery.

Step 8: The Close

When would you like delivery?

It sounds like we have a new client, thank you.

What would you like me to do next? (My favorite)

Step 9: Timeline for Implementing

The new client must have an understanding about what happens next, what could be called a future reality factor. If the prospect get confused, or loses their excitement, they may stop the sale. This also partially addresses "fear of change".

A Client Calendar must be available, and explained, step-by-step, showing them dates on what they have just purchased will be delivered or implemented. It gives the prospect a secure feeling on the decision to be a client.

You cannot just tell them. Put it in writing and show them.

Step 10: Referrals – ask and you generally get.

There is an extremely close relationship between the items checked as "Need Improvement" on the Commonality of Issues Sheet and your sales. The prospect is checking off which items are their hot buttons. They are telling you what items interest them – They are telling you how to close them.

First time users of this process get so excited to find that prospects have no objections to filling out the Commonality of Issues Sheet that they flub on even doing the Recall System. The reason is simple. This is the first time that they find themselves truly engaged with their prospect, and in the excitement they lose their place. I mention this as a cautionary tale.

I hope this information helps you, and your new clients. I can be reached through the website: http://www.rapidsalessuccess.com

ABOUT THE AUTHOR

I am the winner of numerous sales and sales management awards in the medical surgical area, and business services area. I live with my wonderful wife, Catherine, in the Phoenix, Arizona area.

Business-wise, I participate heavily on Linkedin.com, and I'm a member of many different sales related, education related and psychology related groups.

Currently, I am working on a book entitled, *Mental Reflexes®* for a university group.

Figure 1

Our Human
Resources, Inc.

Human
Resources &
Benefits

Payroll &
Workers
Compensation

Your Administrative &
Human Resources Departments

www.ingramcontent.com/pod-product-compliance
Lightning Source LLC
Chambersburg PA
CBHW071436200326
41520CB00014B/3724